Christmas
with KATHIE LEE

*A Treasury of Holiday Stories,
Songs, Poems, and Activities for Little Ones*

Kathie Lee Gifford

Illustrated by Teri Weidner, Susan Calitri, Jesse Clay, and the Alvin S. White Studio

Disney
PRESS

New York

The author's proceeds from this book will go to Childhelp USA.
Childhelp USA® is in the forefront of the fight against child abuse, and operates the Childhelp National Child Abuse Hotline, 1-800-4-A-Child®, which is staffed twenty-four hours daily with professional crisis counselors. Childhelp USA also operates treatment facilities and foster care programming. For more information regarding Childhelp USA, please contact the Childhelp USA National Headquarters, 15757 N. 78th Street, Scottsdale, AZ 85260. (602) 922-8212. www.childhelpusa.org

Grateful acknowledgment is made to Tillie Scarritt for her help in creating the craft activities for this book.

Verses for "The First Christmas" are taken from *The Living Bible*, copyright © 1971. Used by permission of Tyndale House Publishers, Inc., Wheaton, Illinois 60189. All rights reserved.

"The Day Before the Night Before Christmas" is used by permission of James Shock.

Illustration credits:
Teri Weidner illustrated the following selections: "The First Christmas," "Away in a Manger," "The Night Before Christmas," "An Alphabet of Christmas," "Jingle Bells," "Christmas Cookies and Treats," "Up on the Housetop," "Deck the Halls," "The Twelve Days of Christmas," "Christmas Secrets," "Barnaby, the Christmas Elf," "A Christmas Fairy Tale," and "Celebrations Around the World."

Susan Calitri illustrated the following selections: "Happy Birthday, Jesus!" "Decorating the Tree with Ornaments You Can Make," "The Angel Tree," "The Day Before the Night Before Christmas," "Decorating Your House for Christmas," "The Small One Goes to Bethlehem," and "Simple Gifts to Make."

The Alvin S. White Studio provided the illustrations for "Winnie the Pooh's Christmas."

Jesse Clay provided the illustrations for "The Small One."

Photo credits:
Page one: used by permission of Steve Friedman and Buena Vista Television, copyright © 1992. All other photos are from Kathie Lee Gifford's personal collection.

Design by Dragonfly Design, Inc.

Material on pages 6, 7, 8, 19, 30, 31, 84, 85–91; and introductions on pages 9, 13, 14, 16, 18, 20, 27, 32, 34, 38, 46, 48, 56, 60, 62, 74, 78, 82 copyright © 1997 Lambchop Productions, Ltd.

All other material copyright © 1997 by Disney Enterprises, Inc.

Printed in the United States of America.

First Edition
1 3 5 7 9 10 8 6 4 2

Library of Congress Cataloging-in-Publication Data
Gifford, Kathie Lee, 1953–
Christmas with Kathie Lee: a treasury of holiday stories, songs, poems, and activities for little ones/Kathie Lee Gifford. —1st ed.
p.   cm.
Includes index.
ISBN 0-7868-3157-X
1. Christmas. I. Title.
GT4985.G45   1997
394.2663—dc21   97-13492

This book is lovingly dedicated
to the Babe of Bethlehem,
a living, breathing, joyful presence
in the cradle of my heart.

—K. L. G.

Contents

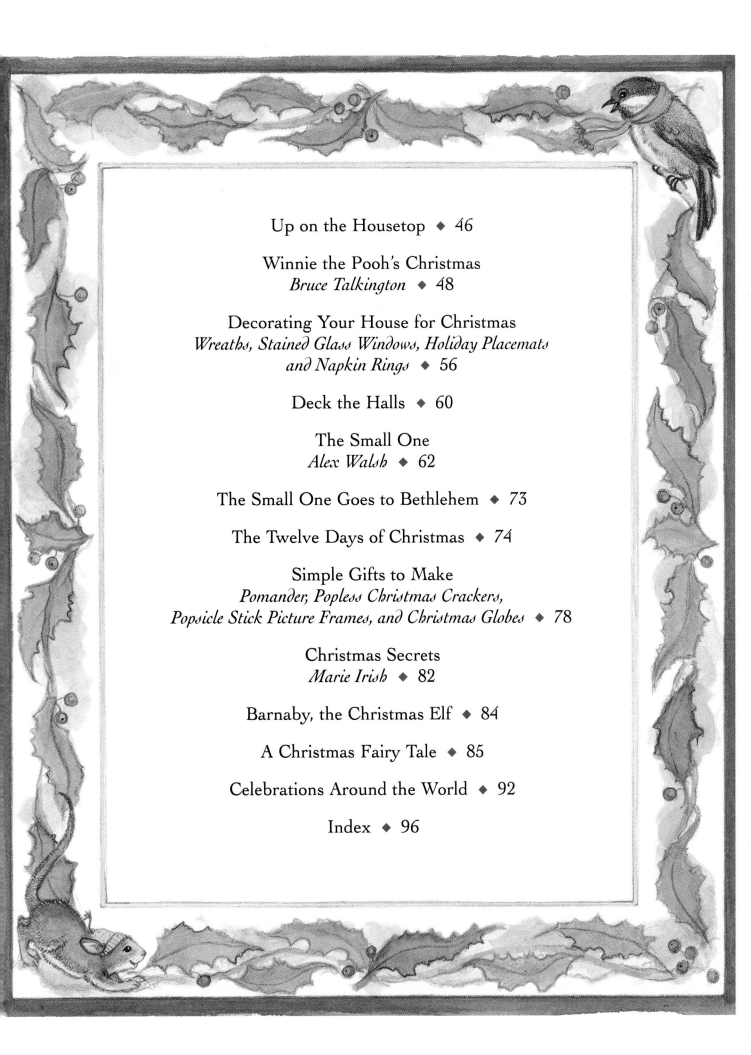

Celebrate Christmas

Christmas. Just the word alone conjures up a joyous symphony of sounds, smells, tastes, traditions, memories, and emotions. It means something different to children than to adults; it is something sacred to millions, and to millions of others, it is a secular season to rest from the labors of a long year. For everyone, it is a reason to celebrate.

Christmas seems to be the only time of the year when the secular and the sacred come together naturally and comfortably. One moment you can steal a kiss under the mistletoe, and the next your soul can swell with joy as you listen to Handel's *Messiah*.

Frank, Cody, and I with our beloved bichons in 1991

Christmases past somehow always seem simpler and dearer than the one we face this year. There is so much to do, so many plans to make, and ultimately so many people to disappoint if things don't go as planned. Because there are so many expectations, there are also equal amounts of frustration, anxiety, and stress. What if we don't order the cards on

Enjoying Christmas in Colorado in 1995

time? What if we get someone the wrong present? What if the weather's bad and we have to cancel the party? It's endless.

But far more poignant are the painful realities that many face during the Christmas season. What if I can't afford food for my children, much less presents? What if a loved one is ill and dying? What if I'm alone? What if I'm homeless while others are singing "I'll Be Home for Christmas"?

So, for me, there is always a conflict of emotions as I approach the holiday season. I am completely overwhelmed by my blessings while at the same time I am acutely aware of the inequities and the injustices of the world.

I try to be careful not to indulge in the excesses of the season and not to overlook the *reason* for our celebration.

The truth, for me, is that Christmas is really a birthday party. A birthday party that first took place some two thousand years ago in a stable in Bethlehem.

A loving brother on Christmas day

For God so loved the world that he sent his greatest gift: his son, so that by the example of his life we could learn how to live our own lives . . . lovingly, kindly, unselfishly, forgivingly.

These are all words that basically are ignored today. "You've got to be tough . . . make the sale . . . grab that advantage . . . win the prize . . . get what you want . . . at any cost." But the costs are often huge. All we have to do is look at our society to see what greed gives birth to.

Now that I have given birth myself I look at everything differently. I don't see Christmas as an opportunity to give my children more things. I see Christmas as an opportunity to show them more love, spend more time with them, and create more memories with them. I'd like to teach them that the true spirit of Christmas is a Life Force for the whole year ahead of them.

For by receiving love I believe we learn how to love. I pray that this Christmas you and your loved ones will share a joy that passes all understanding. And that even in the midst of the tinsel and the toys you will find God's special love.

The First Christmas

from *The Living Bible*

Most people are familiar with the King James version of the Christmas story. But The Living Bible offers a fresh, contemporary account of the birth of Jesus, and children find it easier to understand. Any way the story is told, it continues to thrill our hearts and ignite our imaginations.

About this time Caesar Augustus, the Roman Emperor, decreed that a census should be taken throughout the nation.

Everyone was required to return to his ancestral home for this registration. And because Joseph was a member of the royal line, he had to go to Bethlehem in Judea. He took with him Mary, his fiancée, who was obviously pregnant.

And while they were there, the time came for her baby to be born; and she gave birth to her first child, a son. She wrapped him in a blanket and laid him in a manger, because there was no room for them in the village inn.

That night some shepherds were in the fields outside the village, guarding their flocks of sheep. Suddenly an angel appeared among them, and the landscape shone bright with the glory of the Lord. They were badly frightened, but the angel reassured them.

"Don't be afraid!" he said. "I bring you the most joyful news ever announced, and it is for everyone! The Savior—yes, the Messiah, the Lord—has been born tonight in Bethlehem! How will you recognize him? You will find a baby wrapped in a blanket, lying in a manger!"

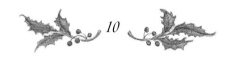

Suddenly the angel was joined by a vast host of others—the armies of heaven—praising God:

"Glory to God in the highest heaven," they sang, "and peace on earth for all those pleasing him."

When this great army of angels had returned again to heaven, the shepherds said to each other, "Come on! Let's go to Bethlehem! Let's see this wonderful thing that has happened, which the Lord told us about."

They ran to the village and found their way to Mary and Joseph. And there was the baby, lying in the manger. The shepherds told everyone what had happened and what the angel had said to them about this child. All who heard the shepherds' story expressed astonishment, but Mary quietly treasured these things in her heart and often thought about them.

At about that time some astrologers from eastern lands arrived in Jerusalem, asking, "Where is the newborn King of the Jews? For we have seen his star in far-off eastern lands, and have come to worship him."

Entering the house where the baby and Mary his mother were, they threw themselves down before him, worshiping. Then they opened their presents and gave him gold, frankincense, and myrrh. Their joy knew no bounds!

Happy Birthday, Jesus!

When Cody was born, he changed our lives. And, of course, he changed the way we celebrated Christmas. All of a sudden, there was no sleeping in! Part of the challenge of raising children is making sure they understand the importance and significance of the holidays we celebrate. We wanted to ensure that from his earliest memory he would understand the true meaning of the season. Children understand birthday parties, and few occasions are as exciting as their own birthday. So we decided to have a party each year to celebrate Jesus's birthday. This keeps the emphasis on the spiritual while maintaining the sense of fun the season brings.

Here are some simple ways to throw the party:

◆ Make a birthday cake that says "Happy Birthday, Jesus." An angel food cake with commercial frosting is easy for young children to ice and decorate.

◆ With your children, set up the Christmas creche on the party table.

◆ Decorations for the party could include red and green balloons and other Christmas-themed accents.

◆ Play games, such as "Pin the tail on the donkey."

◆ Just as the Wise Men brought gifts to the Baby, the children are asked to bring gifts, too. This usually involves donating their toys to children less fortunate. They could collect the toys and deliver them themselves to a local toy drive.

Away in a Manger

Martin Luther

This simple, poignant song is one of my childhood favorites. It reminds us of the humanity of the birth of Jesus . . . how humble a place he first laid his head . . . and how typically his mother loved him, cradled him, and sang him gently to sleep.

Away in a manger,   no crib for a bed.   The little Lord Jesus laid down his sweet head.   The stars in the sky

looked down where he lay,   The little Lord Jesus   asleep in the hay.

Tenderly

1. A - way in a man - ger, no crib for a bed, The lit - tle Lord
2. The cat - tle are low - ing, the ba - by a - wakes, But lit - tle Lord
3. Be - neath me Lord Je - sus I ask thee to stay, Close by me for -
4. A - way in a man - ger, no crib for a bed, The lit - tle Lord

Je - sus laid down his sweet head. The stars in the sky_____ looked
Je - sus, no cry - ing he makes. I love thee, Lord Je - sus, look
ev - er and love me I pray. Bless all the dear chil - dren in
Je - sus laid down his sweet head. The stars in the sky_____ looked

down where he lay, The lit - tle Lord Je - sus, a - sleep in the hay.
down from the sky, And stay by my cra - dle till morn - ing is nigh.
thy ten - der care And take us to hea - ven to live with thee there.
down where he lay, The lit - tle Lord Je - sus, a - sleep in the hay.

Decorating the Tree with Ornaments You Can Make

Trimming the tree is perhaps the most universal of Christmas traditions. Whether your tree ultimately ends up looking like Martha Stewart's or Charlie Brown's doesn't matter. It's a joyous time of togetherness in which the whole family can participate, especially when you make the decorations yourselves!

Clay Ornaments

Children love playing with clay or dough. This recipe makes a wonderful soft clay that can be cut with cookie cutters or shaped by hand. The finished product is air-dried until hard and then can be decorated with tempera or watercolor paints and markers.

Materials:
1 cup of cornstarch
1 cup of baking soda
1¼ cups of cold water
Saucepan and spoon
Paints

Recipe for Clay:

◆ Help your child mix ingredients together in a saucepan.

◆ Stir over medium heat for about five minutes or until the mixture thickens like oatmeal.

◆ Remove from heat and cool on a plate until you can work it with your hands.

◆ Make the desired shape.

◆ Punch a hole with a nail or pencil before the clay begins to harden.

◆ Let air-dry on a cookie rack for two days.

◆ Paint as desired.

Handprint Ornaments

◆ Take an oval-shaped piece of clay, slightly larger than your child's hand.

◆ Flatten the clay with a rolling pin to about a half-inch thickness.

◆ Let your child make a handprint in the clay!

Cookie Cutter Ornaments

◆ Using seasonal cookie cutters of your choice, cut shapes from a flattened piece of clay. Be sure to make a hole for ribbon or string at the top.

◆ Let dry and paint.

Pinecone Ornaments

This project combines collecting and decorating.

Materials:
- Pinecones
- Glue
- Glitter
- Sequins
- Screw eyes
- Ribbon

◆ Paint the pinecones with glue.

◆ Hold a glue-covered pinecone over a dish or pie pan and have your child sprinkle glitter and/or sequins onto the pinecone. For more messy fun, you can also drizzle poster paint.

◆ To hang the pinecones, glue a small screw eye at the top of the pine cone and thread with ribbon.

Yarn Ornaments

This simple project is always unique in its outcome!

Materials:
- White glue
- Wax paper
- Yarn
- Glitter

◆ Mix one cup of white glue with ¼ cup of water.

◆ Use a piece of wax paper as a work surface.

◆ Cut pieces of yarn at least six inches long.

◆ Dip the yarn into the glue mixture.

◆ Remove the yarn from glue mixture and lay it on the wax paper in a random shape.

◆ Sprinkle with glitter and let dry.

The Angel Tree

The concept
of the Angel Tree is a
simple one: you don't have
to be an angel to act like one! Christmas is a time of giving and
in such a needy world there are endless opportunities to brighten the lives of those who
are less fortunate. Right after Thanksgiving is a good time to create your personal
Angel Tree from needs within your community.

Instructions

◆ Trace the angel pattern on this page. Cut out the pattern and lay it on a piece of cardboard. Use the pattern to draw as many angels as you would like.

◆ Add velvet or any other fabric and glue it on top of the cardboard. Decorate with crayons or sparkles or anything you like to individualize the angels. (Cotton is great for angel hair!)

◆ Identify areas of need in your community, e.g., singing to the elderly at a retirement home or sending someone there a Christmas card; helping a needy family with Christmas presents or inviting them for Christmas dinner; visiting the children's ward at a hospital or participating in Toys for Tots in your area. Contact your local church or United Way for suggestions, and make sure you include choices suitable for each family member.

◆ Write an idea on each angel and arrange them on a wall or door in a Christmas tree shape. Or hang them on your Christmas tree. Then have fun choosing which angel you want to be!

The Night Before Christmas

Clement C. Moore

Everyone enjoys the classic poem by Clement C. Moore. So give it a contemporary spin: try reciting it to a rap beat!

'Twas the night before Christmas, when all through the house,
Not a creature was stirring, not even a mouse;
The stockings were hung by the chimney with care,
In hopes that Saint Nicholas soon would be there;

The children were nestled all snug in their beds,
While visions of sugarplums danced in their heads;
And Mama in her kerchief, and I in my cap,
Had just settled our brains for a long winter's nap—

When out on the lawn there arose such a clatter,
I sprang from my bed to see what was the matter.
Away to the window I flew like a flash,
Tore open the shutters and threw up the sash.

The moon on the breast of the new-fallen snow
Gave a lustre of midday to objects below;
When what to my wondering eyes should appear,
But a miniature sleigh and eight tiny reindeer.

With a little old driver, so lively and quick

I knew in a moment it must be Saint Nick!

More rapid than eagles his coursers they came,

And he whistled and shouted and called them by name:

"Now, Dasher! now, Dancer! now, Prancer and Vixen!

On, Comet! on, Cupid! on, Donder and Blitzen!

To the top of the porch, to the top of the wall!

Now dash away, dash away, dash away all!"

As dry leaves that before the wild hurricane fly,
When they meet with an obstacle, mount to the sky,
So up to the housetop the coursers they flew,
With a sleigh full of toys—and Saint Nicholas, too.

And then in a twinkling I heard on the roof
The prancing and pawing of each little hoof.
As I drew in my head, and was turning around,
Down the chimney Saint Nicholas came with a bound.

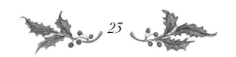

He was dressed all in fur from his head to his foot,
And his clothes were all tarnished with ashes and soot;
A bundle of toys he had flung on his back,
And he looked like a peddler just opening his pack.

His eyes—how they twinkled! his dimples, how merry!
His cheeks were like roses, his nose like a cherry;
His droll little mouth was drawn up like a bow,
And the beard on his chin was as white as the snow.

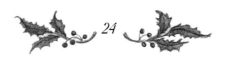

The stump of a pipe he held tight in his teeth,

And the smoke it encircled his head like a wreath.

He had a broad face and a little round belly

That shook, when he laughed, like a bowl full of jelly.

He was chubby and plump—a right jolly old elf;

And I laughed, when I saw him, in spite of myself.

A wink of his eye and twist of his head

Soon gave me to know I had nothing to dread.

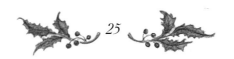

He spoke not a word, but went straight to his work,
And filled all the stockings; then turned with a jerk,
And laying his finger aside of his nose,
And giving a nod, up the chimney he rose.

He sprang in his sleigh, to his team gave a whistle,
And away they all flew like the down of a thistle;
But I heard him exclaim, ere he drove out of sight:
"Happy Christmas to all, and to all a good night!"

An Alphabet of Christmas

Traditional

Children love doing their ABCs and they love Christmas, so little ones really enjoy this project: encourage them to come up with their own!

A for the Animals out in the stable.

B for the Babe in his manger for cradle.

C for the Carols so blithe and gay.

D for December, the twenty-fifth day.

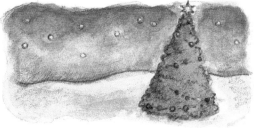

E for the Eve when we're all so excited.

F for the Fire when the Yule log is lighted.

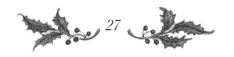

G is the Goose which you all know is fat.

H is the Holly you stick in your hat.

I for the Ivy, which clings to the wall.

J is for Jesus, the cause of it all.

K for the Kindness begot by this feast.

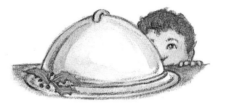

L is the Light shining far in the East.

M for the Mistletoe. Beware where it hangs!

N is the Noel the angels first sang.

O for the Oxen, the first to adore him.

P for the Presents wise men laid before him.

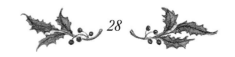

Q for the Quiet that comes in the night,
as stars in the heavens shine joyously bright.

R for the Romps and the Raisins and nuts.

S for the Stockings that Santa Claus stuffs.

T for the Times we always will treasure.

U is for Us, sharing Christmas together.

V for the Visitors, happy boys and girls.

W for Wishes for peace in our world.

X is for Xmas, the day Jesus was born.

Y for Yuletide, the season we adore.

Z for Zzzzzs, as children sleep tight,
resting until Christmas morning's first light.

Christmas in My Family

Like all children, I looked forward with eager glee to the Christmas holidays. We had barely swallowed our last bite of Thanksgiving turkey before we would drag out the old Christmas albums and fill the house with holiday music. Andy Williams, Nat King Cole, Barbra Streisand, and the Carpenters never left the house until well after New Year's!

My niece and nephew in 1984

Christmas at my sister's house in 1988

We certainly didn't have much money to spare, but we decorated the house with pinecones, holly, and evergreens from our yard. I loved crafts, so I would contribute some new handmade item every year. I'm sure it wasn't professional-looking, but my parents always feigned delight at my efforts and proudly displayed them everywhere!

Every year my mom would make *klinga* for Christmas morning. This delicate Swedish sweet was just perfect on a cold December day with the fire popping and all the wrappings at our feet.

Cody looks hopefully at his stocking in 1996

It's funny, I don't remember *any* of the presents I received, but I remember so well the feelings of warmth and love, all of the smells of the crackling fire and the evergreen tree, the delicious taste of klinga, and the overwhelming sense of wonderment of being a child at Christmastime. These are the kinds of treasures I hope my own children will remember.

Cassidy tells Santa her secrets in 1996

31

Jingle Bells

Traditional

Every kid knows and loves this ageless little song. Children also like to make up their own versions — the sillier the better!

Brightly

1. – Dash - ing thro' the snow in a one horse o - pen sleigh, –
2. A day or two a - go I— thought I'd take a ride, And
3. – Now the ground is white, – Go it while you're young, –

O'er the fields we go, – Laugh - ing all the way;— –
soon Miss Fan - nie Bright Was seat - ed by my side;— The
Take the girls to - night, And sing this sleigh - ing song;— Just

Bells on bob - tail ring, — Mak - ing spir - its bright, What
horse was lean and lank, Mis - for - tune seem'd his lot, He
get a bob - tailed nag, Two - for - ty for his speed, Then

fun it is to ride and sing A sleigh - ing song to - night!
got in - to a drift - ed bank, And we, we got up - sot.
hitch him to an o - pen sleigh, And crack! you'll take the lead.

Jin - gle, bells! jin - gle, bells! Jin - gle all the way!

Oh, what fun it is to ride in a one - horse o - pen sleigh!—— one - horse o - pen sleigh!

Christmas Cookies and Treats

Frank jokes that I need a map to find my own kitchen. But even though I usually try to spend as little time in the kitchen as possible, Christmastime is the exception. Nothing's more fun than making cookies together—except maybe eating them.

Sugar Cookies with Crushed Candy

These are sparkly Christmas cookies that young children love to make. Don't forget to leave some out for Santa!

Materials:
- Sugar cookie dough
- Rolling pin
- Clear hard candy in a variety of colors
- Cookie cutters
- Wax paper

Recipe for sugar cookie dough:
- 1 cup sugar
- 1 cup margarine
- 1 large egg
- ½ teaspoon vanilla extract
- 1½ teaspoons baking powder
- ½ teaspoon salt
- 2½ cups flour

◆ In a large bowl, cream margarine and sugar.

◆ Add the egg, vanilla extract, baking powder, salt, and flour. Beat well.

◆ On a floured board, knead dough by hand. Wrap the dough in plastic wrap or wax paper and refrigerate for a few hours, until firm.

◆ Once your dough is ready to be cut out, use the rolling pin to crush the hard candy, being careful not to mix the colors.

◆ Roll out the dough to about a quarter-inch thickness and cut into shapes with cookie cutters.

◆ Place dough cutouts on wax paper on the cookie sheet and sprinkle the crushed candy on the cookies in any festive design.

◆ Bake in an oven at 350° for ten to twelve minutes or until brown.

Apple-Coconut Snowman

Frosty, watch out!

Materials:
   Toothpicks
   3 apples:
      1 large apple, such as a
         baking apple
      1 medium apple, such
         as a McIntosh
      1 tiny apple, such as a
         crab apple or love apple
   Commercial icing (vanilla) or
      homemade buttercream frosting
   Unsweetened coconut
   Raisins
   Hard candy

◆ Dip apples in icing.

◆ Using the toothpicks, assemble the snowman.

◆ Shake the coconut over the icing.

◆ Decorate with raisin eyes and candy.

Graham Cracker Gingerbread House

Children can have a lot of fun with this since there is no right or wrong way to build them. The houses can be as elaborate as you desire—the basic elements are graham crackers, icing, and candy decorations.

Materials:
    One box of graham crackers
    A pint-size milk carton (for
      support)
    Commercial icing in a tin (or
      homemade)
    Christmas candy such as
      peppermint sticks, candy
      canes, and gumdrops

◆ Use about six cookies for each house.

◆ Use the icing as glue, and adhere the cookies to the sides of the milk carton.

◆ Put the candies on the outside of the house to suggest windows and doors.

Christmas Tree Cookies

These are delicious and delightful cookies; however, they do require a lot of adult participation.

Materials for cookie dough:
- 1½ cups all-purpose flour, sifted
- ½ cup butter or margarine
- ¼ cup sugar
- ½ teaspoon ground cinnamon
- 2–3 tablespoons grated orange zest
- 1 egg yolk

Materials for decoration:
- 2 cups confectioners' sugar, sifted
- 2–3 tablespoons orange juice
- Coarsely grated orange zest

◆ Preheat the oven to 350°.

◆ Place the flour into a bowl and mix in the butter until the mixture resembles bread crumbs. Add the sugar, cinnamon, orange zest, and egg yolk, and mix to a smooth dough.

◆ Knead lightly, then roll out on a lightly floured surface to about a quarter-inch thickness. Using a cookie cutter, cut out Christmas tree shapes. Place on the baking sheets about two inches apart and bake for ten to fifteen minutes, until golden. Transfer to a wire rack to cool.

◆ Mix the confectioners' sugar with the orange juice until smooth, and use it to coat the tops of the cookies. Sprinkle with orange zest.

The Day Before the Night Before Christmas

James Shock

A few years ago, a gentleman named James Shock sent us this poem he had written for his own family. Frank and I were charmed by it, and our children loved it, too. It's nice to know that even elves aren't perfect!

It was two days before Christmas, one silly December,
And this is what happened—as I do remember. . . .

A year they had rested, but this was the day . . .
Saint Nick and I tested the deer and the sleigh.
The flight had gone well, when we noticed nearby,
A gaggle of birds who were hogging the sky.

Saint Nick blew the horn on the sleigh so they'd know,

They flew in our path and were flying too low.

The birds didn't hear it, and kept to their course—

Saint Nick and I shouted, until we were hoarse.

Then all of a sudden, and quick as a flash,

The birds and the reindeer met with a CRASH!

The deer were quite startled by what had occurred.

They'd never in flight, even once, hit a bird.

So startled, in fact, they forgot how to fly,

And the sled began falling right out of the sky.

It looked rather grim until Santa saved all

By popping the parachute, stopping our fall.

The sleigh slowly drifted around and around . . .

And made a loud THUMP as it bumped on the ground.

The air bag burst out of the dash with a BANG,
As wipers were waggling and sirens now rang.
The seat belt, well fastened, had held me in place;
For Santa, poor fellow, that wasn't the case.

Santa shot from the sled and fell deep in the snow,
And Rudolph cracked up the bulb in his nose.
The sleigh was a wreck, and would need lots of fixin',
As would the antlers, now crooked, on Vixen.
I pulled Santa out, but he couldn't stand still.
He shivered and shook in the cold arctic chill.

Upon our return to make needed repairs,
Saint Nick hung his soggy suit over some chairs.
He then said, "I feel like I'm getting the flu,
The sleigh is a wreck, and I've washing to do."
I told him I'd help him—he must go to bed.
"That's kind of you, Herman," he smiled and said.

I wanted to tell him, but didn't know how,
I'd never done laundry, at all, before now.
"You sure you can do it?" I heard Santa ask.
"Of course!" I assured him. "I'll tackle this task."

I went to the laundry and found a machine,
And stuffed the suit in, with detergent, to clean.
The temperature setting, I thought, should be HOT!
The hotter the water, the cleaner it got?!?

The white of its trim needed bleach, so I guessed.
I poured in a little, then dumped in the rest.
It happened so quickly, before I could blink,
Like magic, before me, bright red turned to pink.

That wasn't the worst, for the suit I now saw,
Besides being pink was, at present, quite small.
I didn't know laundry, but this much I knew,
My job at the North Pole would surely be through.

I trembled with fear as I knocked at his door,

While waiting to show the result of my chore.

The door slowly opened and there stood Saint Nick,

All wrapped in a blanket, still looking quite sick.

His beard rolled in curlers to ready his hair,

He looked at the suit and said, "What have you there?"

I told him . . . then noticed his face showed a smile,

He said, "In some countries I bet it's in style."

Then he turned to his wife: "Dear, what do you think?"

She slyly replied, "Only real men wear pink."

A blush arose quickly and filled his round face.

"Your heart," chuckled Santa, "was in the right place."

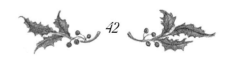

With that mess behind me, I went on my way,
To fix Rudolph's nose from the crash of the sleigh.
I searched for a bulb of bright red I could use,
But all I could find were some greens and some blues.
Since green was the brightest and best I could find,
I didn't think Rudolph or Santa would mind.

I took to the stable the bulb that I chose,
And then fit the socket on top of his nose.
His eyes crossed together to stare at the light,
While other deer giggled and laughed at the sight.
Since Rudolph had been through their teasing before,
He found them much easier, now, to ignore.

I went home to bed where I'd stay out of trouble,
And ran the next day to Saint Nick's on the double.

Santa was happy I'd paid him a visit.
He said, "I need help," and I said, "What is it?"
He told me he needed a hand getting dressed,
If he was to squeeze in the suit I had messed.

In order to fit his big belly within,
He'd borrowed a girdle to keep it held in.
The girdle was tight, and he grunted and groaned.
The suit *had* to fit—it was all Santa owned.
I knew if it didn't, there might be no trip;
My strength nearly doubled, and up went the *zzzzzip*!

Saint Nick had the suit on, but it didn't look right.
Pale legs were showing, and it was too tight.
He peeked in the mirror, then put on his hat,
And asked if I thought the suit made him look fat.
I told him the children all liked him that way,
And that made him happy, I'm happy to say.

When the elves brought the reindeer and sled to his door,
Saint Nick saw the nose on the leader for sure.
"This night, we're a sight," he laughed when he said,
"They'll think it's Saint Pat who took flight in my sled."

I told him that nose was the best I could do,
But if he'd prefer I could change it to blue.
He told me as long as it guided our way,
A green nose would work, and we climbed in the sleigh.

So come Christmas Eve when you look in the sky,
Indeed, you believe, you see Santa go by—
Perhaps it's the shuttle, perhaps, no one knows . . .
But if what you spy has a blinking green nose,
There's one way to know if it is what you think—
Just look for a driver dressed tightly in pink.
You'll know in an instant, if that's what you see:
You've just spotted Rudolph, and Santa, and me!

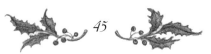

Up on the Housetop

Traditional

Preschoolers love to act out songs with hand motions. "Up on the Housetop" is a favorite because kids love to "click, click, click." Here are the motions for the refrain:

Repeat

Ho, ho, ho!

Who wouldn't go!

Up on the housetop

click, click, click,

Down through the chimney
with good Saint Nick.

Brightly

1. Up on the house-top—— rein-deer pause, Out jumps good old San-ta Claus;
2. First comes the stock-ing of lit-tle Nell; Oh, dear San-ta, fill it well;

Down through the chim-ney with lots of toys, All for the lit-tle ones, Christ-mas joys.
Give her a dol-lie that laughs and cries, One that will o-pen and shut her eyes.

Ho, ho, ho! Who would-n't go! Ho, ho, ho! Who would-n't go!——

Up on the house-top, click, click, click, Down through the chim-ney with good Saint Nick.

47

Winnie the Pooh's Christmas

Bruce Talkington

Young children love Winnie the Pooh because they can identify with his confusions and fears (not to mention that he forgets to put on his pants every day!). In this story, Winnie the Pooh is perplexed by the use of stockings and the need for Christmas gifts for his friends in the Hundred-Acre Wood. All is resolved happily, of course, with the reassuring idea that sometimes the simplest gifts are the best.

It was the night before Christmas, and Winnie the Pooh's nose was pressed flat against a windowpane. He was gazing out at the snow hushing the Hundred-Acre Wood, gathering cozily like bedclothes around the house where he lived.

All at once Pooh heard a rattle of very small knocks at his front door. He opened the door to find a very small snowman with a pair of very Piglet-looking ears.

"May I come in?" it asked.

"Please do," said Pooh.

The snowman stood shivering in front of the fire and, with every tremble and quiver, began to look less and less like a snowman and more like Piglet!

"Why, hello, Piglet!" blurted Pooh, delighted to see his very small, very best friend standing in a puddle of water.

"My!" breathed Piglet in wonder as he gazed up at Pooh's Christmas tree. "You did a fine job decorating your tree. Perhaps you could use some help wrapping up presents?"

"But, Piglet," said Pooh, "the gifts won't be here until tomorrow morning. And then I unwrap them. That's the way it's done, you know." There may have been a few things about Christmas on which Pooh was a little hazy, but opening presents wasn't one of them.

"No, Pooh, I mean I'll help you wrap the presents you're going to give!" said Piglet.

Pooh's smile disappeared. "Oh!" he said quietly. "*Those* gifts." Then even more quietly, he added, "Oh bother!"

"What's the matter, Pooh?" Piglet asked.

Pooh sighed tremendously. "I think I forgot something," he said. "It's presents."

"No presents?" Piglet looked up at Pooh sadly. "Not even a very small one?"

Pooh shook his head. "I'm sorry, Piglet."

Piglet smiled bravely. "It's all right, Pooh. It's the thought that counts, you know," he sniffed. "I think I'll go home now."

Pooh saw his friend to the door and watched him walk sadly down the path.

"Oh my," Pooh said to himself as he stepped out into the snow. "If it's the thought that counts at Christmas, I think I'd better ask Christopher Robin what he thinks about thoughts and presents and Christmas and everything."

It was a long, chilly tramp through the

swirling night. Pooh was very glad when he arrived at Christopher Robin's house, and he knocked loudly on the door.

"Pooh Bear!" Christopher Robin exclaimed. "Come in!"

Pooh was led into Christopher Robin's toasty den. "My!" Pooh breathed. "This certainly looks like Christmas! So I suppose I can ask you what I came to find out," he said, "as soon as I remember what it is."

But then Pooh frowned and stepped up to Christopher Robin's fireplace, where a row of socks and stockings of all shapes and sizes hung neatly from the mantelpiece.

"Don't you think," Pooh remarked, "that Christmas is, perhaps, not the best time for drying your laundry?"

"Silly old bear," Christopher Robin laughed. "That's not laundry. They're stockings to hold Christmas presents!"

"You mean," Pooh answered, "you have to have stockings to put presents in?"

"Yes," said Christopher Robin, "that's the way it's done."

"Oh bother!" said Pooh. Not only did he not have presents for his friends, but they had no stockings to put the presents in!

When Pooh mentioned this, Christopher Robin laughed. "Come with me, Pooh Bear. I have plenty of stockings for everyone."

Christopher Robin showed Pooh a drawer containing socks of every size, shape, and color. "These are all stockings who have lost their mates and would love to have someone with whom to share Christmas," said Christopher Robin. "It's the thought that counts, you know."

"Why, yes," replied Pooh, happy that Christopher Robin had remembered to answer the question that he had forgotten to ask. "Thank you very much, Christopher Robin."

Soon Pooh was walking happily home with his arms full of stockings.

"It is very late, and I must get these stockings delivered." He considered for a moment. "I must get everyone presents, too, of course, but the stockings come first."

And so Pooh crept into his friends' homes one by one and left a stocking, with a little note "From Pooh" hanging from each one's mantel.

First, of course, there was Piglet's house, where Pooh placed a very small stocking.

He then left a striped one for Tigger because he was sure that was the sort of stocking Tiggers like best.

Pooh left a very bright orange one at Rabbit's house.

Eeyore got the warmest and friendliest stocking Pooh could find.

Gopher received a long, dark stocking. Pooh thought it was what a tunnel would look like if a tunnel were a stocking.

Finally, Owl was given a stocking the color of the sky—in which, Pooh thought, he would like to fly if he were Owl.

It was very, very late when Pooh nailed his own honey-colored stocking to his very own mantelpiece.

"Now that this stocking business is all taken care of," said Pooh, settling down in his softest armchair. "I simply must do some serious thinking about what I am going to give my friends for Christmas." Pooh closed his eyes, and soon neither his snoring nor the sun rising over the Hundred-Acre Wood disturbed his thoughts.

In fact, Pooh did not wake up until a knock sounded at his door, accompanied by a chorus of "Merry Christmas, Pooh Bear!"

Pooh opened his eyes and glanced about anxiously. "Oh no!" he thought. "My friends are here for Christmas and I have no presents for any of them!

"There's only one thing to do. I shall simply have to tell my friends I'm sorry, but I only thought about presents for them."

Pooh opened his door and in rushed all his friends, all thanking Pooh at once for his thoughtful gifts.

Piglet was wearing a new stocking cap. "My ears are very grateful, Pooh Bear. It was exactly what I wanted."

Tigger told Pooh how much he loved his new "stripedy" sleeping bag. "It's cozier than cozy!"

Rabbit couldn't wait to tell him how he'd always dreamed of owning a color-coordinated carrot cover. How could Pooh possibly have known?

Gopher appreciated the "bag" for toting around his rock samples. Eeyore explained—if anyone was interested—that his tail had never been warmer than in its new warmer.

Owl was positive his brand-new wind sock would provide him with all the necessary data required to prevent the occasional crash landing through his dining room window!

Pooh put his hands behind his back and looked thoughtful. "Something awfully nice is going on, though I'm not at all sure how it happened."

"I'll tell ya how it happened, buddy bear," exclaimed Tigger. "It's called Christmas!"

Everyone presented Pooh with a pot of honey.

"Christmas," sighed Pooh happily. "What a very sweet thought, indeed!"

Decorating Your House for Christmas

Decorating for the holidays is half the fun of enjoying them. Making it a family affair only increases the fun—from hanging a simple wreath on the front door to elaborate boughs along the staircase, it doesn't matter how much or how little you do, as long as you do it together. Think of your house as a movie set, setting the scene for the drama to come!

All of the crafts here are easy for young children to make.

Wreaths

Wreaths are always a fun project because of the variations on a theme. Here are three ideas that are easy and enjoyable for young children.

Clay Wreath

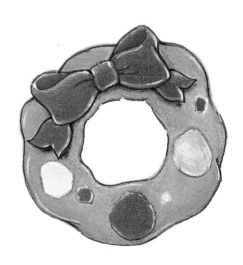

◆ Using the clay recipe on page 16, wreaths both large and small can be made easily by using circles of various sizes.

◆ As an alternative to painting a dried clay wreath, you can gently press sequins and glitter into the clay wreath prior to drying.

Paper Plate Wreath

◆ Cut a circle out of the center of a paper plate.

◆ Decorate the outer circle.

◆ Decorating suggestions: markers, crayons, or paints; pre-cut leaves or torn green construction paper with cut red paper or ribbon to signify berries; a bow might be a nice finishing touch.

◆ Hang by a string or ribbon.

Cardboard Wreath

For a larger wreath, you might try this.

◆ Cut the wreath from a piece of cardboard (for example, a pizza box).

◆ Punch a hole at the top and tie a length of yarn or ribbon through the hole, to be used for hanging later.

◆ Pour white glue into a small cup (small yogurt cups work well). You will also need a glue brush for applying the glue to the cardboard.

To decorate your wreath:

◆ Use colored tissue paper torn and rolled into small balls and pressed onto the glued cardboard.

◆ Try popcorn!

◆ Colored pasta: if you want to color pasta, mix food color and rubbing alcohol in equal parts and put the mixture in a plastic bag. Put pasta in the bag and shake. Use a variety of pasta shapes, if you like. Then place on a baking sheet in the oven at 200° until dry. You can also use plain, uncolored pasta and spray it with gold paint after your child has glued it to the wreath.

Stained Glass Windows

You can hang these decorations anywhere—on a doorknob, or in a window, of course.

Materials:
   Crayons (grated into separate
      bowls)
   Wax paper cut into 6" x 12"
      pieces (12" or whatever the
      width of the wax paper is)
   Colored poster board
   Yarn or string
   Stapler
   Hole puncher
   Scissors
   Iron

◆ Grate the crayons separately using a bowl for each color. I suggest using purple, blue, green, red, yellow, and orange.

◆ Sprinkle the crayon shreddings—in the desired arrangement— over half of the 6" x 12" wax paper. Fold the other half over.

◆ Iron lightly, just enough to melt the crayon.

◆ Cut poster board frames, two each, to fit the desired shape: diamond, square, circle, triangle, etc. Make sure that the 6" x 6" square window will be covered.

◆ Sandwich the stained glass in the poster board frame. Staple in a few places.

◆ Punch one or two holes at the top of the frame, and hang it with string or yarn.

◆ You may decorate the frames as well, if you like—either with markers, watercolors, or by gluing on glitter, sequins, or buttons. However, these windows are beautiful on their own!

◆ As an alternative to the crayon-melt technique, glue strips of colored tissue paper on wax paper and place in the frames as above. Also, some craft stores sell colored cellophane, which can be cut by children or adults into any shape they desire. These shapes can then be placed on clear contact paper, which is then folded over and placed in frames as above.

Holiday Placemats and Napkin Rings

This is a simple project that always gets a lot of "oohs" and "ahhs."

Materials for Holiday Placemats:
    Old Christmas cards
    Clear contact paper
    Oaktag or construction paper

◆ Arrange cards onto placemat-sized oaktag or construction paper.

◆ Cover with clear contact paper.

◆ It's especially fun to put similar cards together, such as all the Santa cards or angel cards.

Materials for Napkin Rings:
    Paper tubes
    Cloth or gift wrap scraps
    Glue
    Scissors or pinking shears—if desired

◆ A grownup cuts the tube into sections about an inch wide. If you decide to use pinking shears, cut the fabric and paper into small pieces, about 1" x 1".

◆ Glue the pieces and press them in place to cover the tubes, inside and out.

◆ Glue bits of yarn, lace braid, or feathers for decoration. Nuts and evergreen sprigs make nice seasonal touches.

Deck the Halls

Traditional Welsh

*"Deck the Halls" is one of our family's favorites.
It's such a joyous, happy song, and kids sure love
the "fa-la-la" parts.*

Joyfully

1. Deck the hall with boughs of hol - ly, Fa la la la la, la la la la.
2. See the blaz - ing yule be - fore us, Fa la la la la, la la la la.
3. Fast a - way the old year pass - es, Fa la la la la, la la la la.

'Tis the sea - son to be jol - ly, Fa la la la la, la la la la.
Strike the harp and join the cho - rus, Fa la la la la, la la la la.
Hail the new, ye lads and lass - es Fa la la la la, la la la la.

Don we now our gay ap - par - el, Fa la la la la la la la la.
Fol - low me in mer - ry meas - ure, Fa la la la la la la la la.
Sing we joy - ous, all to - geth - er Fa la la la la la la la la.

Troll the an - cient Yule - tide car - ol. Fa la la la la, la la la la.
While I tell of Yule - tide trea - sure. Fa la la la la, la la la la.
Heed - less of the wind and weath - er. Fa la la la la, la la la la.

The Small One

Alex Walsh

I don't know exactly how "The Small One" came into our lives. I just remember my son, Cody, introducing it to me one night and loving every moment of it. As a mother I am constantly on my guard about what my children eat, think, watch, say, and do. We live in a violent, often selfish world where "sentimental" is deemed corny and "spiritual" means ignorant. We seem to have lost our heart. But Small One reminds us that there is no greater love than being willing to lay down one's life for a friend. What a wonderful message for today's world—and for today's children.

Once long ago there was a little boy who lived outside a town called Nazareth. His father owned four donkeys. Three of the donkeys were young and strong. The fourth donkey was old and weak. But the boy loved him best of all. The donkey's name was Small One.

Each day the boy brought food and water to all the donkeys. But Small One was the only donkey he played with. Small One was his friend.

One day the boy was going to help his father gather firewood. "Are the donkeys ready yet?" his father called.

The boy was feeding Small One. "Almost, Father," he replied. "Hurry up," he said to the little donkey.

The boy and his father took the four donkeys and went over the hill to gather firewood. The father walked in front with the three strong donkeys. The boy walked behind, leading Small One. As they went about their work, the boy tried to find the lightest pieces of wood. He knew that Small One was too old and weak to carry a heavy load.

Meanwhile, the boy's father was putting heavy pieces of wood onto the backs of the other three donkeys. He saw that his son was putting only little sticks on Small One's back. He did not like it, but he said nothing.

When it was time to go home, the boy pushed Small One up a hill. The little donkey was very tired.

All of a sudden there was a *crash*! Small One had slipped down the hill and dropped the firewood. The boy hurried to pick up the wood. He put a few pieces on Small One's back and carried the rest himself.

When the boy reached the top of the hill with the little donkey, his father was waiting for him. He was angry.

"Don't you have enough work to do without doing Small One's, too?" he said.

"Oh, Father . . . he is no trouble at all. I don't mind," said the boy.

As they walked home, the father spoke to the boy. "Son, Small

One can no longer carry a load big enough to pay for his food."

The boy put his arms around Small One's neck.

"He is just a little tired today, Father," he said. "His strength will come back."

"No, he is old, my son. His strength is gone. We cannot afford to keep him any longer."

The boy grabbed his father's arm. "No, Father . . . you don't mean that!"

The father put his arms around the boy.

"I am sorry, Son, but tomorrow I must take Small One to town and sell him. He will bring a piece of silver."

The boy began to cry. "No, Father, no!" he said. "You can't sell him. You can't!"

"Please, Son, try to understand," said his father. "Small One is old. He should not have to work so hard. In town he will have an easier life. You must be strong."

As his father turned away, the boy said quietly, "May I take him to town?"

"Very well," said his father. "You can leave in the morning and be home by nightfall. But understand . . . Small One *must* be sold."

"Yes, Father," the boy replied sadly.

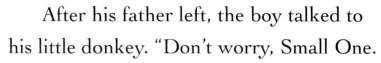

After his father left, the boy talked to his little donkey. "Don't worry, Small One. You won't have to carry these heavy sticks anymore. And I won't sell you to just anyone. He will be someone special, someone who will feed you and brush your coat and love you as I do."

The little donkey was very sad.

"Somewhere there is a special friend for you," the boy went on. "And somehow we will find him."

The donkey licked the boy on the nose.

"Good night, Small One," said the boy as he covered the donkey up for the night.

The next day the boy and Small One walked over the hills to town. Soon they came to the gates. The town was a very busy

place. The boy and the donkey felt very small amid the legs of tall horses and camels and the wheels of many carts.

At the gates the boy and Small One were stopped by a guard.

"What do you want, boy?" he asked.

"I have come to sell my donkey, sir," said the boy.

The guard looked at Small One and laughed. "I know a man who is in need of such an animal," he said. "Go to the third shop inside these gates."

"Oh, thank you, sir," said the boy.

The boy and Small One found the shop and went inside. It was very dark, and it smelled bad. Some other animals were tied up inside. They looked frightened.

"Now don't be afraid, Small One," said the boy.

They looked around. At first they did not see anyone. Then they saw a man sharpening a knife.

"Hello," called the boy.

The man came toward them.

"Yes?" he said.

The boy said nothing.

"Do you have a donkey to sell?" asked the man.

"Yes . . . his name is Small One," the boy replied.

"I will give you one piece of silver."

"Will you take good care of him?"

The man was surprised.

"I only want his hide, boy. I am a tanner."

"You want to make leather out of him!" the boy cried.

"One piece of silver," repeated the tanner.

"No, no, I won't sell him!" shouted the boy as he and Small One ran out of the shop.

The boy and the donkey ran through the streets. When they were far from the tanner's shop, they stopped to catch their breath.

"I'm sorry, Small One," said the boy. The little donkey licked him.

Small One and the boy walked through the marketplace. They saw a potter working at his wheel.

"Would you like to buy my donkey?" asked the boy.

"Not that sorry bag of bones," said the potter.

Then the boy saw a baker.

"Would you buy my donkey?" he asked.

"Not that scrawny little beast," said the baker. "Since my wife is so fat, I think I should buy a horse, at least."

"Doesn't anybody need a donkey?" the boy asked three merchants who were passing by.

"Take our advice," they said. "You will never find a buyer here. Go see the horse trader, three blocks straight ahead."

The boy took Small One over to the horse trader's stand. The trader was selling a beautiful horse for fifty pieces of silver.

"Please, sir, would you sell my donkey?" asked the boy as he led Small One up the ramp.

The man took a look at Small One and laughed and laughed. He decided to make fun of the little donkey.

"Look at this beautiful animal,"

he said to the crowd. "Who will pay one thousand pieces of silver for him?"

Everyone laughed.

"But you can see that he is as strong as a bull," the horse trader continued as he got on Small One's back.

At first the poor little donkey was almost flattened by the weight.

"Get off!" shouted the boy.

But then Small One gathered all his strength and tossed the man high into the air. The horse trader landed in a heap on the ground.

"Get that miserable beast out of here!" he shouted to the boy, who rushed away with the donkey.

Small One and the boy walked slowly through the streets. The tired donkey knew there was only one solution. He led the boy back to the tanner's shop, ready to give up his life to help the boy. They were both very sad.

The boy sat down in the street and cried. He put his arms around Small One's neck. Suddenly he heard a man's voice.

"Tell me, son, are you the owner of this small donkey? I need a gentle animal to carry my wife, Mary, to Bethlehem. Is he for sale?"

The boy looked up at the man's friendly face.

"Yes, sir," he said.

"What do you call him?"

"Small One," replied the boy, smiling.

"Well, he looks strong enough."

"And kind," said the boy.

The man smiled. "I can offer you only one piece of silver," he said. "I know it is very little."

The boy felt he could trust the man. "Oh, that's fine!" he said. "I just want Small One to have a good home."

"Well, my son, he will," said the man, rubbing the donkey's head. "I will take good care of him." Then he gave the boy the piece of silver.

The boy gave his friend one last hug. "Good-bye, Small One. Be strong and sure of foot and follow your new master."

"Come along, Small One," said the man as he turned to go. Then the little boy climbed high atop the town wall to wave good-bye to the man, his wife, and Small One as they began their journey to Bethlehem.

The boy felt sad and happy at the same time. He was certain that Small One would have a good life with his new family.

The Small One Goes to Bethlehem

Help Small One bring Mary and Joseph to Bethlehem.

The Twelve Days of Christmas

Traditional

Traditionally, the twelve days of Christmas fall between December 25 and January 6. In our house, we love to perform the song with friends, making each person act out their day. It's really funny as each participant tries to outdo the others!

1 On the first day of Christmas
My true love sent to me
A partridge in a pear tree.

2 On the second day of Christmas
My true love sent to me
Two turtle doves, and
A partridge in a pear tree.

3 On the third day of Christmas
My true love sent to me
Three French hens,
Two turtle doves, and
A partridge in a pear tree.

4 *On the fourth day of Christmas*
My true love sent to me
Four calling birds,
Three French hens,
Two turtle doves, and
A partridge in a pear tree.

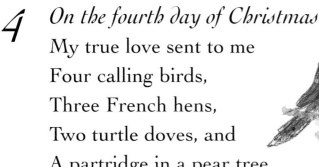

5 *On the fifth day of Christmas*
My true love sent to me
Five gold rings,
Four calling birds,
Three French hens,
Two turtle doves, and
A partridge in a pear tree.

6 *On the sixth day of Christmas*
My true love sent to me
Six geese a-laying,
Five gold rings,
Four calling birds,
Three French hens,
Two turtle doves, and
A partridge in a pear tree.

7 *On the seventh day of Christmas*
My true love sent to me
Seven swans a-swimming,
Six geese a-laying,
Five gold rings,
Four calling birds,
Three French hens,
Two turtle doves, and
A partridge in a pear tree.

8 *On the eighth day of Christmas*
My true love sent to me
Eight maids a-milking,
Seven swans a-swimming,
Six geese a-laying,
Five gold rings,
Four calling birds,
Three French hens,
Two turtle doves, and
A partridge in a pear tree.

9 *On the ninth day of Christmas*
My true love sent to me
Nine drummers drumming,
Eight maids a-milking,
Seven swans a-swimming,
Six geese a-laying,
Five gold rings,
Four calling birds,
Three French hens,
Two turtle doves, and
A partridge in a pear tree.

10 *On the tenth day of Christmas*
My true love sent to me
Ten pipers piping,
Nine drummers drumming,
Eight maids a-milking,
Seven swans a-swimming,
Six geese a-laying,
Five gold rings,
Four calling birds,
Three French hens,
Two turtle doves, and
A partridge in a pear tree.

11 *On the eleventh day of Christmas*
My true love sent to me
Eleven ladies dancing,
Ten pipers piping,
Nine drummers drumming,
Eight maids a-milking,
Seven swans a-swimming,
Six geese a-laying,
Five gold rings,
Four calling birds,
Three French hens,
Two turtle doves, and
A partridge in a pear tree.

12 *On the twelfth day of Christmas*
My true love sent to me
Twelve lords a-leaping,
Eleven ladies dancing,
Ten pipers piping,
Nine drummers drumming,
Eight maids a-milking,
Seven swans a-swimming,
Six geese a-laying,
Five gold rings,
Four calling birds,
Three French hens,
Two turtle doves, and
A partridge in a pear tree.

Simple Gifts to Make

Several years ago I borrowed an idea from our friends Jerry and Amy Engle that they had used successfully with their own family: each child receives just three gifts, representing the gold, frankincense, and myrrh that the three Wise Men brought for Baby Jesus. This puts an emphasis on quality, not quantity, and keeps Christmas morning far more focused on its true meaning. Instead of the kids' being overwhelmed by so many gifts, each present becomes more special while still preserving the spirit of the first Christmas.

All of the crafts here are easy to make and are wonderful gifts for children to give to parents, grandparents, baby-sitters, and friends.

Cassidy and Cody opening their gifts on
Christmas day, 1996.

Pomander

Preschoolers love the sensory experience of the process of making these with fragrant oranges, lemons, and cloves.

Materials:

Firm, fresh oranges or lemons

Whole dried cloves
Toothpick or pushpin

Nylon net
Ribbon or pretty yarn

◆ A grown-up should poke holes in the orange skin (or lemon skin) with either a toothpick or a pushpin.

◆ Insert a whole clove into each hole. These holes can be random, or it might be fun to create a face or some other design—but try to keep the holes as close together as possible.

◆ For greater fragrance, you can roll the finished pomander in a mixture of cinnamon, allspice, and nutmeg.

◆ Wrap the pomander in a square of nylon net and tie the ends with ribbon. It will shrink and harden as the orange or lemon dries out.

◆ Have your child hang it in a closet or kitchen, or wrap it up to give to a grandparent or special relative.

Popless Christmas Crackers

This is a fast, easy project that kids love. The "pop" is left out to save everyone's eardrums. For some reason, just pulling and opening the ends of these crackers and getting the goody inside is satisfaction enough.

Materials:
Toilet paper roll (empty)
Individually wrapped hard candy, charms, or little plastic toys and figures
Colored tissue paper
Ribbon

◆ Insert the goodies into the toilet paper roll.

◆ Wrap with the tissue paper of your choice and tie the ends with the ribbon!

Popsicle Stick Picture Frames

These make a great gift with a family or school picture inside.

Materials:
Cardboard
Popsicle or craft sticks
White glue
Glue stick
Scissors

◆ Cut cardboard to the desired size. For framing a 5" x 7" print, I suggest a piece about 9" x 7" or 8" x 10" in size. Brown cardboard cut from boxes is best; your child can paint it as desired.

◆ Glue a photo or drawing into the frame using the glue stick.

◆ Help your child arrange the popsicle or craft sticks around the frame—two popsicle sticks for the sides, overlapped with one popsicle stick for the top and one for the bottom—and glue in place around the edges.

◆ Tiny acorns, pinecones, nuts, dried flowers, or glitter can be glued on for decoration. Painting the frame with watercolors is pretty, too.

◆ After these frames are made glue a soda-can pop-top to the back of the frame for hanging on a wall.

◆ For standing the frame upright, however, cut another piece of cardboard in a triangular shape to fit the back of the frame. Fold it in half and glue one side to the frame.

Christmas Globes

Both children and adults become enchanted by Christmas globes. Here is a variation on a theme.

Materials:
> For best results, a hot-glue gun should be used. Please do not let your child use the gun—only an adult should handle it.
> A clean plastic peanut butter container or some other clear container.
> Glitter
> Christmas ornament or plastic figure

◆ Put some glitter in the jar (gold, white, or silver is nice).

◆ Add water.

◆ Attach the ornament or plastic figure to the inside of the cap with the hot-glue gun.

◆ Screw on the cap with ornament attached—tightly.

◆ Turn upside down and you will have your very own Christmas globe!

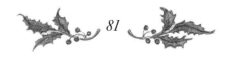

Christmas Secrets

Marie Irish

This poem captures all of the anticipation of Christmas and the fun of giving on Christmas Day.

Think of the thousands of secrets
That are tucked securely away,
All sorts of wonderful secrets
To be revealed on Christmas Day.

Secrets large and secrets small,
Secrets short and secrets tall,
Secrets thick and secrets thin —
Won't the folks who get them grin?

There are secrets flat on their backs,
There are others hanging up high,
Some are standing smack on their heads,
Some in pitchy-black corners lie.

Secrets round and secrets square,
Secrets dark and secrets fair,
Secrets sour and secrets sweet,
Secrets to wear and secrets to eat.

And if all these secrets were one,
And laid out on a long, long shelf,
I think it would surely surprise
Dear old jolly Santa himself.

Barnaby, the Christmas Elf

Sometime during my childhood a new friend arrived and never left! One day, out of the blue, my mother began talking in a saucy tone to someone on the sofa that none of the children could see! Barnaby was his name, she told us, and he was over 700 years old. Santa had sent him to make sure Dave and Michie and I were truly being good, and although this news alone immediately improved our behavior, soon we were all caught up in his presence . . . talking with Barnaby (Mother interpreting, of course) and including him in all our family activities.

Now that I have a young family of my own, Barnaby continues to arrive right after Thanksgiving and to oversee our preparations until right before Christmas, when he returns to Santa's workshop to report on Cody and Cassidy. I'm always a little sad when Barnaby leaves. . . . It's amazing how well behaved they are when he's around!

A Christmas Fairy Tale

Kathie Lee Gifford

I love to tell the children stories that I just make up as I go along. Even I was surprised by "the end" of this one.

Once upon a time, in a far-off land, there lived a beautiful princess. Each day she would sit at her tower window high in the castle and look out at the vast and wondrous world before her, dreaming. Princess Cassidy knew that life held great mystery but also great rewards, and she looked forward to the day when she would meet her destiny. But she also knew that if her dreams were ever to come true, she would have to *make* them come true.

It was Christmas Eve, and she was once again sitting alone at her castle window. All of the preparations for the great Christmas feast were going on without her, but she didn't have the heart to join in the Christmas bustle going on inside the castle.

Suddenly, she noticed a figure on the horizon. It was a man on a stunning stallion, and he was galloping toward the castle gates!

Princess Cassidy took a deep breath, smoothed out the wrinkles of her gossamer gown, and readied herself to meet the mysterious visitor. In a matter of minutes, he stood there before her. The sunlight from her window made his armor shine like silver. Slowly, he walked toward her and gallantly bowed, sweeping his cloak before him.

"Forgive me, sweet Princess, for barging in with no invitation, but with your permission I wish to tell you how I have come to be standing here before you."

"Of course," said the princess. "Won't you sit down?"

"Thank you," smiled the man as he reached for a small chair. "I have traveled for many months. I can hardly believe my journey is finally over."

"Over?" asked the princess. "You mean you came such a long way to see me?" At this, a smile crept to her lips as she offered her visitor some tea.

"Indeed," the man answered. "Please let me explain. Five years ago I was a spoiled, selfish prince. I thought of nothing and no one in my kingdom except myself. In fact, on this very day five years ago, I did not even remember that it was Christmas Eve, and that a prince should be giving gifts to all of his subjects, and planning a merry time with feasting and dancing. I made everyone work on building a new castle for me, because I had tired of the old one. When I thought the work was going too slowly, I became enraged and screamed at the people to work faster and faster. I told them to build me a new stable with hundreds of stalls for all of my horses. I left my subjects no time to celebrate the season. The people were miserable and cursed me behind my back."

"My!" exclaimed Princess Cassidy. "Then what happened?"

"On Christmas Day, as I was walking through the forest, a pinecone fell on my head. Furious, I picked it up to throw it away, when it magically transformed into an elf! I was astonished. He sat in my hand, shook his little finger at me, and said, 'Hey, Prince, if you're ever going to be a real prince then you're going to have to learn to control your temper! And not only that, you're going to have to learn to be loving, fair, generous, and humble, too.'

"I replied, 'But how will I ever learn to be all of those things? I've been this way since the day I was born.'

"The little elf sat down in my palm and looked me straight in the eye. 'I will help you until you become the prince you were meant to be.'"

Princess Cassidy could hardly contain her interest. "And did he?" she asked. "Did the little elf help you?"

"Oh yes," the prince replied. "For the past five years he has been by my side. When I was selfish, he taught me to share. When I was unkind, he taught me to be loving; when I was angry, he taught me to be compassionate; and when I was arrogant, he taught me to be humble.

"To show that I was no longer quite the same prince, I gave a great feast for my subjects on Christmas Day. The next Christmas, I gave everyone a gift—a magical, special gift. For the third Christmas, I spent months traveling across my kingdom, visiting all of the people and finding out what I could do to make their lives better."

"And then," asked the princess, "what did you do next?"

"This past Christmas, I gave everything away—my stables, my castle, and everything in it. The elf said, 'Now, now you are ready. Now I will lead you to your destiny.' It has taken us almost a year to travel here, and we had to slay a dragon along the way. Before we arrived at your castle gate, the elf disappeared. But he led me here—to you, Princess Cassidy."

"To me?" the princess gasped. "But you're not my type!"

Celebrations Around the World

For thousands of years, people around the world have been enjoying festivals and celebrations in December. These midwinter celebrations began many, many years before the birth of Jesus, usually in recognition of the winter solstice, December 21. This is the day that marks the time when daylight hours start to become longer and the nights shorter, as they do every year. Because the sun was so important to many of these peoples' ways of life, they celebrated its rebirth. That is why many December festivities include symbols of light. As the Christian religion joined in with these December celebrations, these symbols also came to represent the light of the Christ Child and the star of Bethlehem.

Here are some Christian traditions from around the world:

In many Christmas Eve church services, candles are used to light up the church.

In northern European countries, a gigantic log called a Yule log is burned during December.

In Italy, France, and Spain, fireworks light up the night sky at Christmastime.

In Ireland, families leave candles lit in the windows of their houses to help guide Mary, Joseph, and Jesus on their way.

In Sweden, people celebrate Saint Lucia's Day during December. The oldest girl in the family gets up early in the morning to make pastries and coffee and deliver them to her parents while they are still in bed. The special pastries that are made for this event are marked with an *X* on them to represent Jesus Christ. The daughter also wears a special costume: a wreath with lighted candles in it and a white dress with a red sash.

Germany is the country where Christmas trees were first used. As in other countries, candles, lights, and stars are used to decorate the tree.

In Mexico, Christmas begins on December 16, the first day of *posadas*. The posadas re-create Mary and Joseph's search for a place to stay in Bethlehem, and people travel from home to home pretending they are Mary and Joseph or the mean innkeeper. Houses are decorated with greens, paper lanterns, and poinsettias. When the posadas are over, a great party is held with food, fireworks, and piñatas.

$\mathcal{M}$any other cultures have celebrations at the end of the year:

$\mathcal{J}$ewish people celebrate Hanukkah in November or December. Hanukkah is the festival of lights, and a special candleholder, called a menorah, is used. There is one candle for each night of Hanukkah.

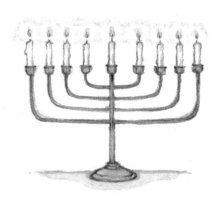

$\mathcal{I}$n India, Hindu people celebrate Divali, the Hindu New Year. Divali is also a festival of lights, and lights symbolize knowledge. Lamps and candles are lit everywhere, and people give each other gifts and cards.

$\mathcal{I}$n the United States, Kwanzaa is celebrated at the end of December. Kwanzaa is not a religious festival like Hanukkah or Christmas, but it is meant to remind African-Americans of their heritage and values. Part of the Kwanzaa celebration includes lighting the *kinara*, a special candleholder that holds seven candles. One candle is lit for each day of Kwanzaa. Each day represents a different African-American ideal, such as faith and community.

Index